### Selected Themes from the Motion Picture

# Harry Potter

### AND THE
## Sorcerer's Stone

**Music by
JOHN WILLIAMS**

**Arranged by
VICTOR LOPEZ**

## Contents

Flute (0645B)
Clarinet (0646B)
Alto Sax (0647B)
Tenor Sax (0648B)
Trumpet (0649B)
Horn (0650B)
Trombone (0651B)

D1003187

Motion Picture Artwork © 2001 Warner Bros.

**WARNER BROS. PUBLICATIONS**
Warner Music Group
An AOL Time Warner Company
USA: 15800 NW 48th Avenue, Miami, FL 33014

 WARNER/CHAPPELL MUSIC

CANADA: 15800 N.W. 48th AVENUE
MIAMI, FLORIDA 33014
SCANDINAVIA: P.O. BOX 533, VENDEVAGEN 85 B
S-182 15, DANDERYD, SWEDEN
AUSTRALIA: P.O. BOX 353
3 TALAVERA ROAD, NORTH RYDE N.S.W. 2113
ASIA: THE PENINSULA OFFICE TOWER, 12th FLOOR
18 MIDDLE ROAD
TSIM SHA TSUI, KOWLOON, HONG KONG

 NUOVA CARISCH

ITALY: VIA CAMPANIA, 12
20098 S. GIULIANO MILANESE (MI)
ZONA INDUSTRIALE SESTO ULTERIANO
SPAIN: MAGALLANES, 25
28015 MADRID
FRANCE: CARISCH MUSICOM
25, RUE D'HAUTEVILLE, 75010 PARIS

 INTERNATIONAL MUSIC PUBLICATIONS LIMITED

ENGLAND: GRIFFIN HOUSE,
161 HAMMERSMITH ROAD, LONDON W6 8BS
GERMANY: MARSTALLSTR. 8, D-80539 MÜNCHEN
DENMARK: DANMUSIK, VOGNMAGERGADE 7
DK 1120 KØBENHAVNK

# HEDWIG'S THEME

**B♭ TENOR SAXOPHONE**

Music by **JOHN WILLIAMS**
*Arranged by* VICTOR LOPEZ

# DIAGON ALLEY

Music by **JOHN WILLIAMS**
*Arranged by* **VICTOR LOPEZ**

\* Try to play the sixteenth notes (stems down); if they are too hard, play eighth notes (stems up).

# HOGWARTS FOREVER

Music by **JOHN WILLIAMS**
*Arranged by VICTOR LOPEZ*

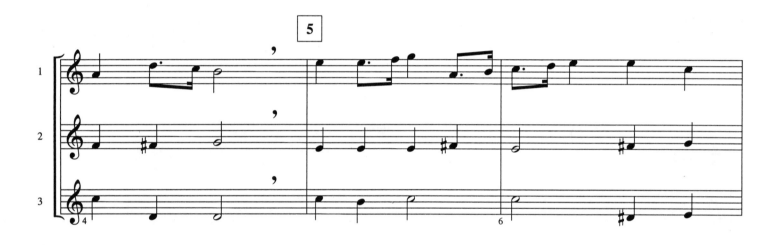

# NIMBUS 2000

Music by **JOHN WILLIAMS**
*Arranged by VICTOR LOPEZ*

# CAST A CHRISTMAS SPELL

Music and Lyrics by **JOHN WILLIAMS**
*Arranged by VICTOR LOPEZ*

# HARRY'S WONDROUS WORLD

Music by **JOHN WILLIAMS**
*Arranged by VICTOR LOPEZ*

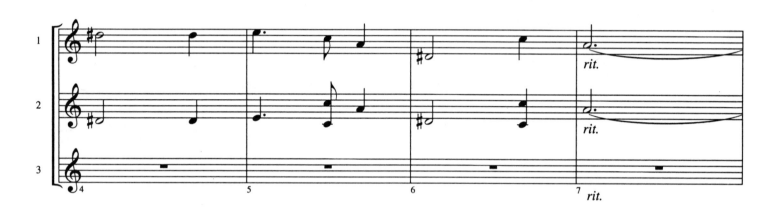

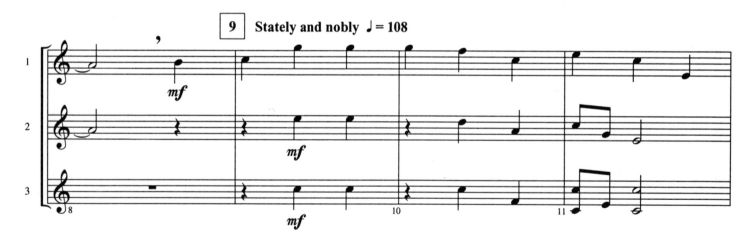

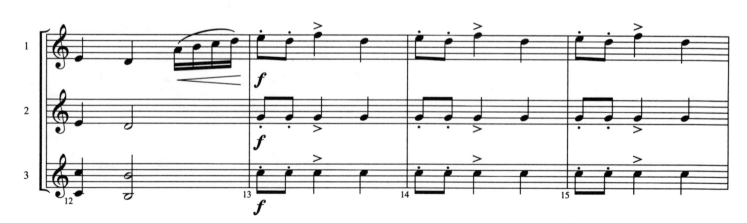

*Gb = F#.

# PARTS OF A TENOR SAXOPHONE
# AND FINGERING CHART

When there are two fingerings given for a note use the first one unless the alternate fingering is suggested.

When two enharmonic notes are given together (F♯ and G♭ for example), they sound the same pitch and are played the same way.

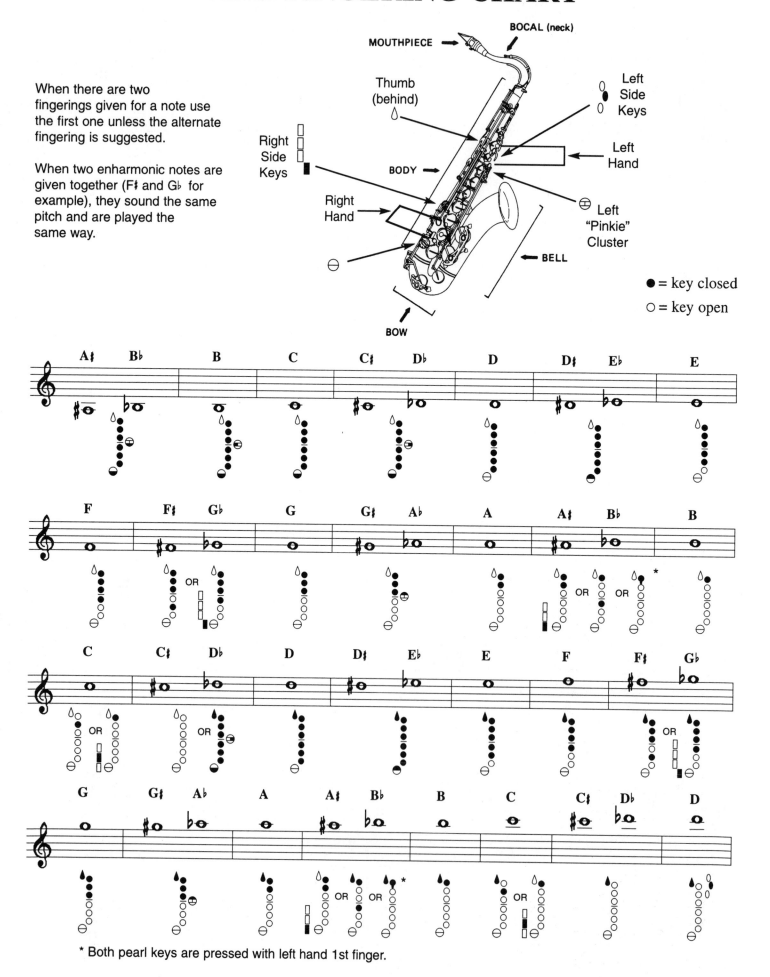

* Both pearl keys are pressed with left hand 1st finger.